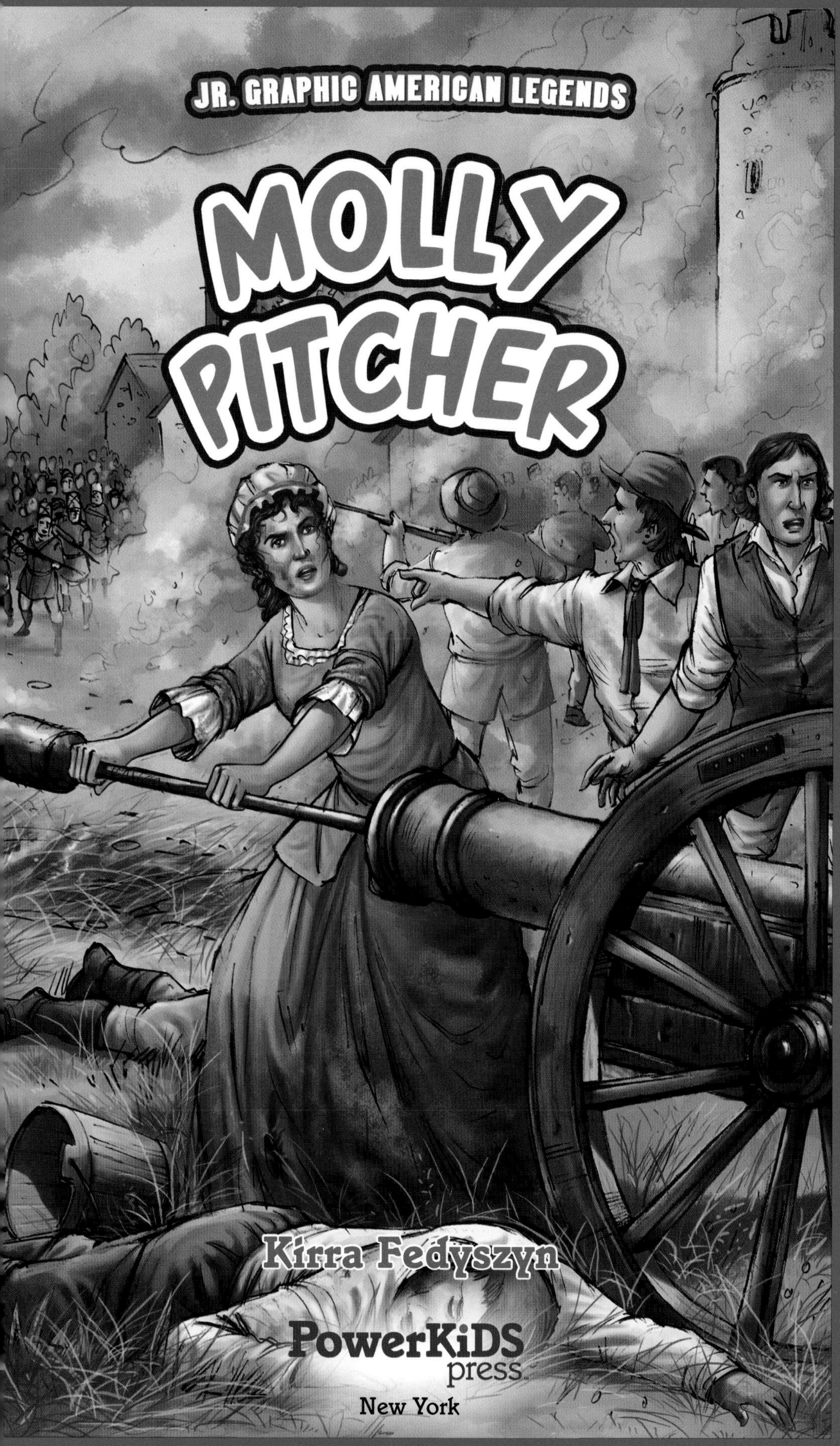

JR. GRAPHIC AMERICAN LEGENDS

MOLLY PITCHER

Kirra Fedyszyn

PowerKiDS press
New York

Published in 2015 by The Rosen Publishing Group, Inc.
29 East 21st Street, New York, NY 10010

First Edition

Editor: Joanne Randolph
Book Design: Contentra Technologies
Illustrations: Contentra Technologies

Library of Congress Cataloging-in-Publication Data

Fedyszyn, Kirra.
 Molly Pitcher / by Kirra Fedyszyn. — First edition.
    pages cm. — (Jr. graphic American legends)
 Includes index.
 ISBN 978-1-4777-7205-8 (library binding) — ISBN 978-1-4777-7206-5 (pbk.) —
 ISBN 978-1-4777-7207-2 (6-pack)
 1. Pitcher, Molly, 1754-1832—Juvenile literature. 2. Monmouth, Battle of,
 Freehold, N.J., 1778—Juvenile literature. 3. Women revolutionaries—United
 States—Biography—Juvenile literature. 4. Revolutionaries—United States—
 Biography—Juvenile literature. 5. United States—History—Revolution, 1775-
 1783—Biography—Juvenile literature. 6. Pitcher, Molly, 1754-1832—Comic
 books, strips, etc. 7. Monmouth, Battle of, Freehold, N.J., 1778—Comic books,
 strips, etc. 8. Women revolutionaries—United States—Biography—Comic
 books, strips, etc. 9. Revolutionaries—United States—Biography—Comic books,
 strips, etc. 10. United States—History—Revolution, 1775-1783—Biography—
 Comic books, strips, etc. I. Title.
 E241.M7F43 2015
 973.3'34092—dc23
 [B]

Manufactured in the United States of America
CPSIA Compliance Information: Batch #WS14PK2: For Further Information contact Rosen Publishing, New York,
New York at 1-800-237-9932

Contents

Introduction

During the **American Revolution**, women could not join the **military**. That did not stop Molly Pitcher from following her husband to war. In the Battle of Monmouth, she brought water to soldiers and took up her husband's cannon when he was **injured**. The bravery of Molly and others like her helped the American colonists defeat the British and create a new nation.

Main Characters

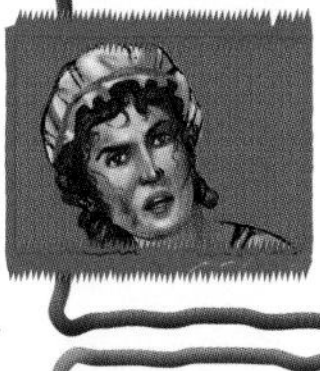

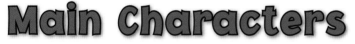

Mary Ludwig Hays McCauly (1754–1832) The daughter of immigrant farmers, Mary, often called Molly, became one of the best-known women in the American Revolution. She followed her husband to war and showed great bravery on the **battlefield** at the Battle of Monmouth.

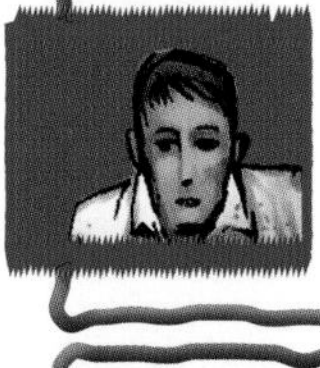

William Hays (?–1789) Molly's first husband, William, was a barber. He enlisted as an artilleryman in the Continental army. When he left home to fight in the war, Molly went with him. He died several years after the war ended as a result of injuries he suffered in battle.

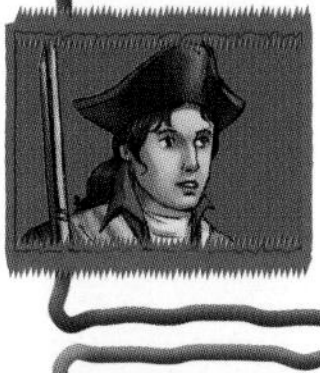

Margaret Corbin (1751–1800) Some believe she was actually the legendary Molly Pitcher. Margaret followed her husband to war and fought in his place when he was killed.

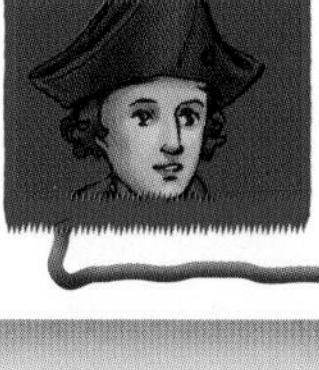

Deborah Sampson (1760–1827) Sampson **disguised** herself as a man to fight in the American Revolution. Her **feminine** appearance earned her the nickname Molly from fellow soldiers.

MOLLY PITCHER

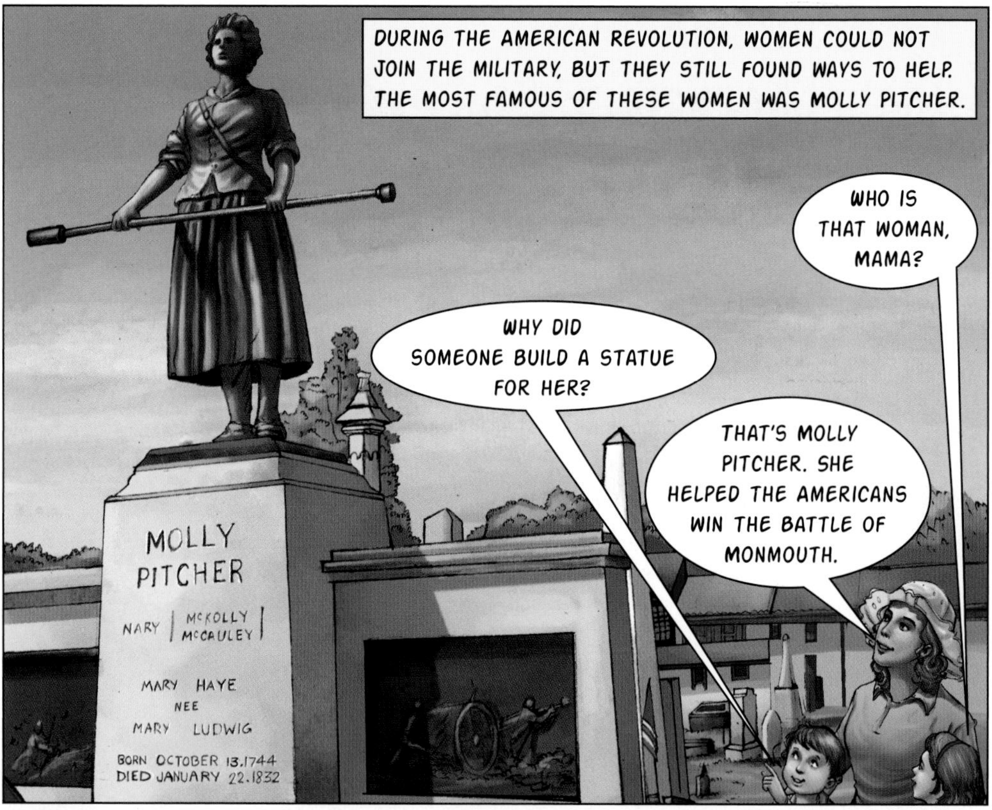

DURING THE AMERICAN REVOLUTION, WOMEN COULD NOT JOIN THE MILITARY, BUT THEY STILL FOUND WAYS TO HELP. THE MOST FAMOUS OF THESE WOMEN WAS MOLLY PITCHER.
WHO IS THAT WOMAN, MAMA?
WHY DID SOMEONE BUILD A STATUE FOR HER?
THAT'S MOLLY PITCHER. SHE HELPED THE AMERICANS WIN THE BATTLE OF MONMOUTH.
MOLLY PITCHER
NARY | McKOLLY | McCAULEY |
MARY HAYE
NEE
MARY LUDWIG
BORN OCTOBER 13.1744
DIED JANUARY 22.1832

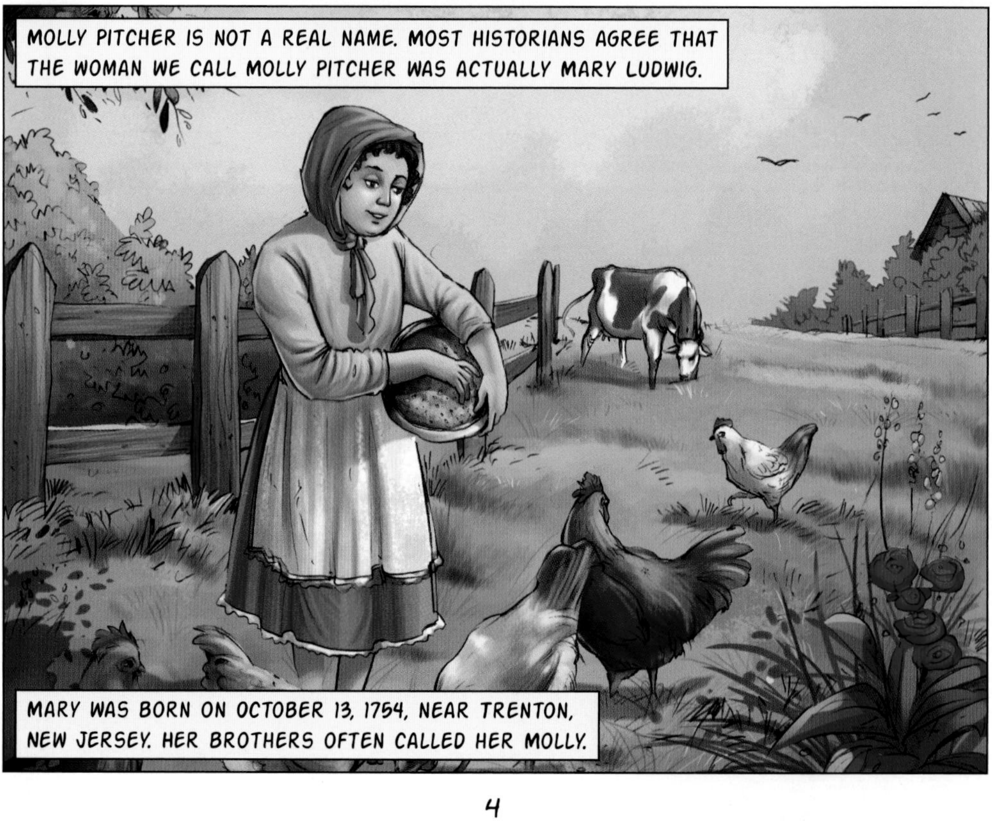

MOLLY PITCHER IS NOT A REAL NAME. MOST HISTORIANS AGREE THAT THE WOMAN WE CALL MOLLY PITCHER WAS ACTUALLY MARY LUDWIG.
MARY WAS BORN ON OCTOBER 13, 1754, NEAR TRENTON, NEW JERSEY. HER BROTHERS OFTEN CALLED HER MOLLY.

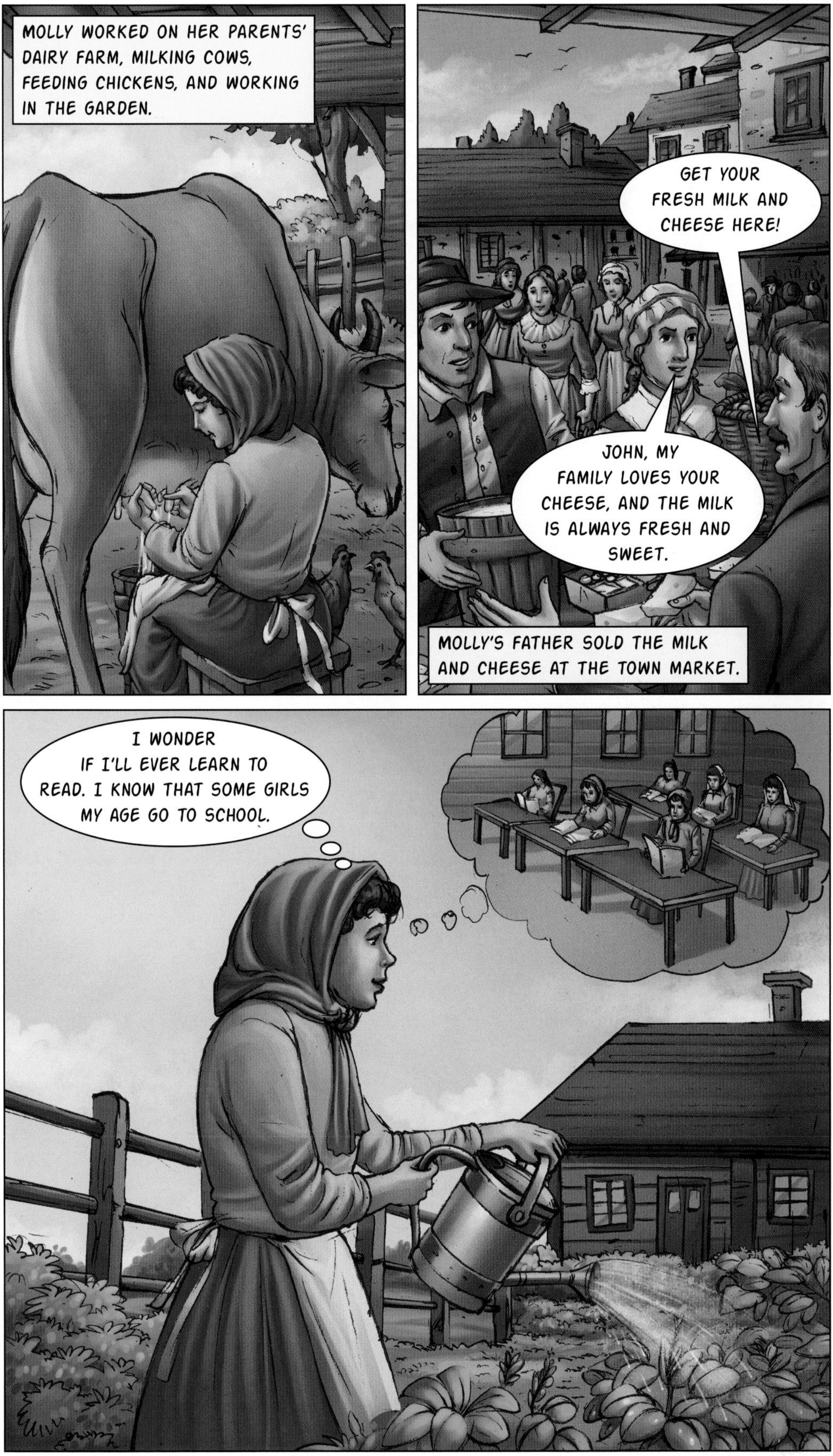
MOLLY WORKED ON HER PARENTS' DAIRY FARM, MILKING COWS, FEEDING CHICKENS, AND WORKING IN THE GARDEN.
GET YOUR FRESH MILK AND CHEESE HERE!
JOHN, MY FAMILY LOVES YOUR CHEESE, AND THE MILK IS ALWAYS FRESH AND SWEET.
MOLLY'S FATHER SOLD THE MILK AND CHEESE AT THE TOWN MARKET.
I WONDER IF I'LL EVER LEARN TO READ. I KNOW THAT SOME GIRLS MY AGE GO TO SCHOOL.

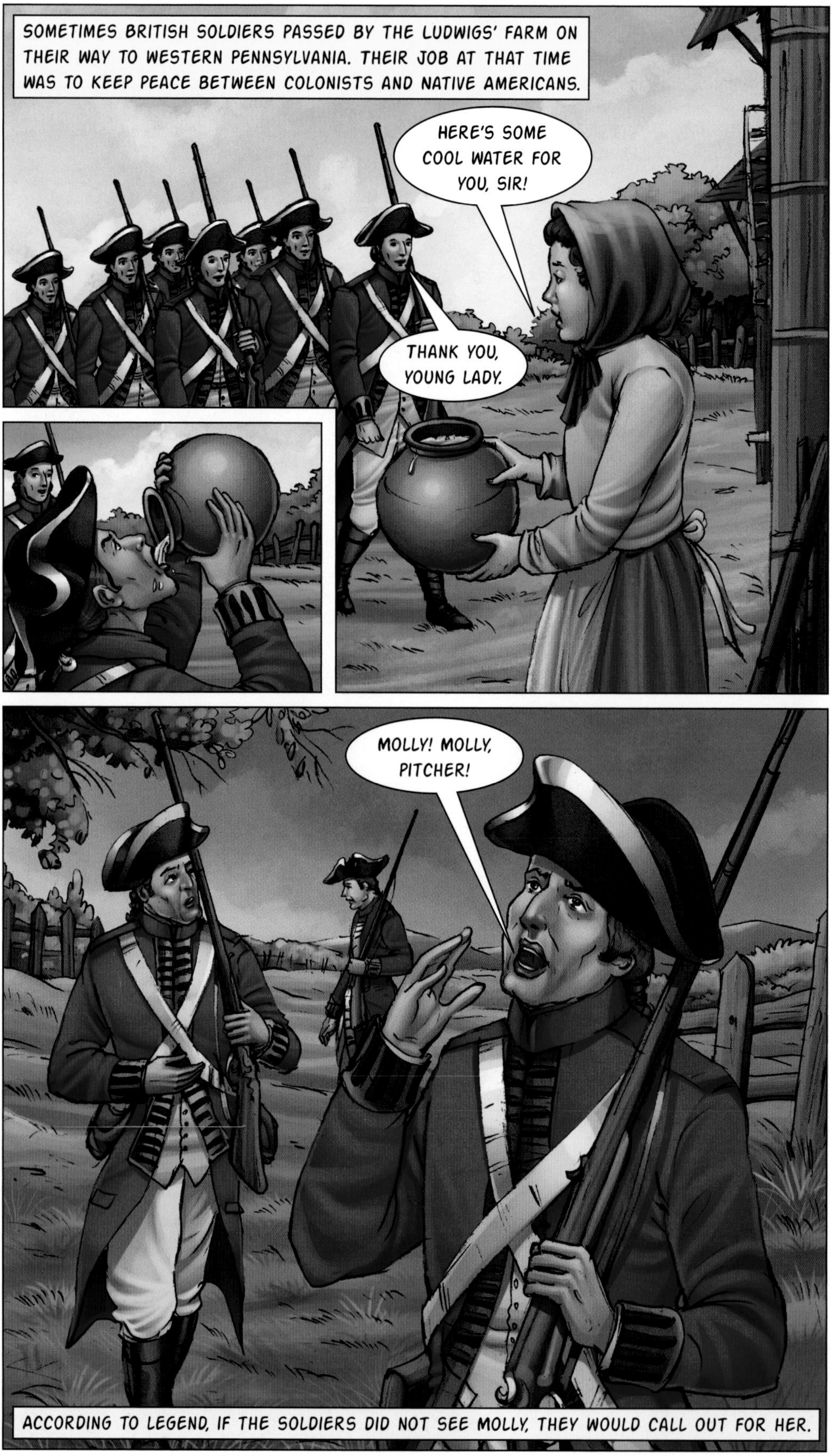
SOMETIMES BRITISH SOLDIERS PASSED BY THE LUDWIGS' FARM ON THEIR WAY TO WESTERN PENNSYLVANIA. THEIR JOB AT THAT TIME WAS TO KEEP PEACE BETWEEN COLONISTS AND NATIVE AMERICANS.
HERE'S SOME COOL WATER FOR YOU, SIR!
THANK YOU, YOUNG LADY.
MOLLY! MOLLY, PITCHER!
ACCORDING TO LEGEND, IF THE SOLDIERS DID NOT SEE MOLLY, THEY WOULD CALL OUT FOR HER.

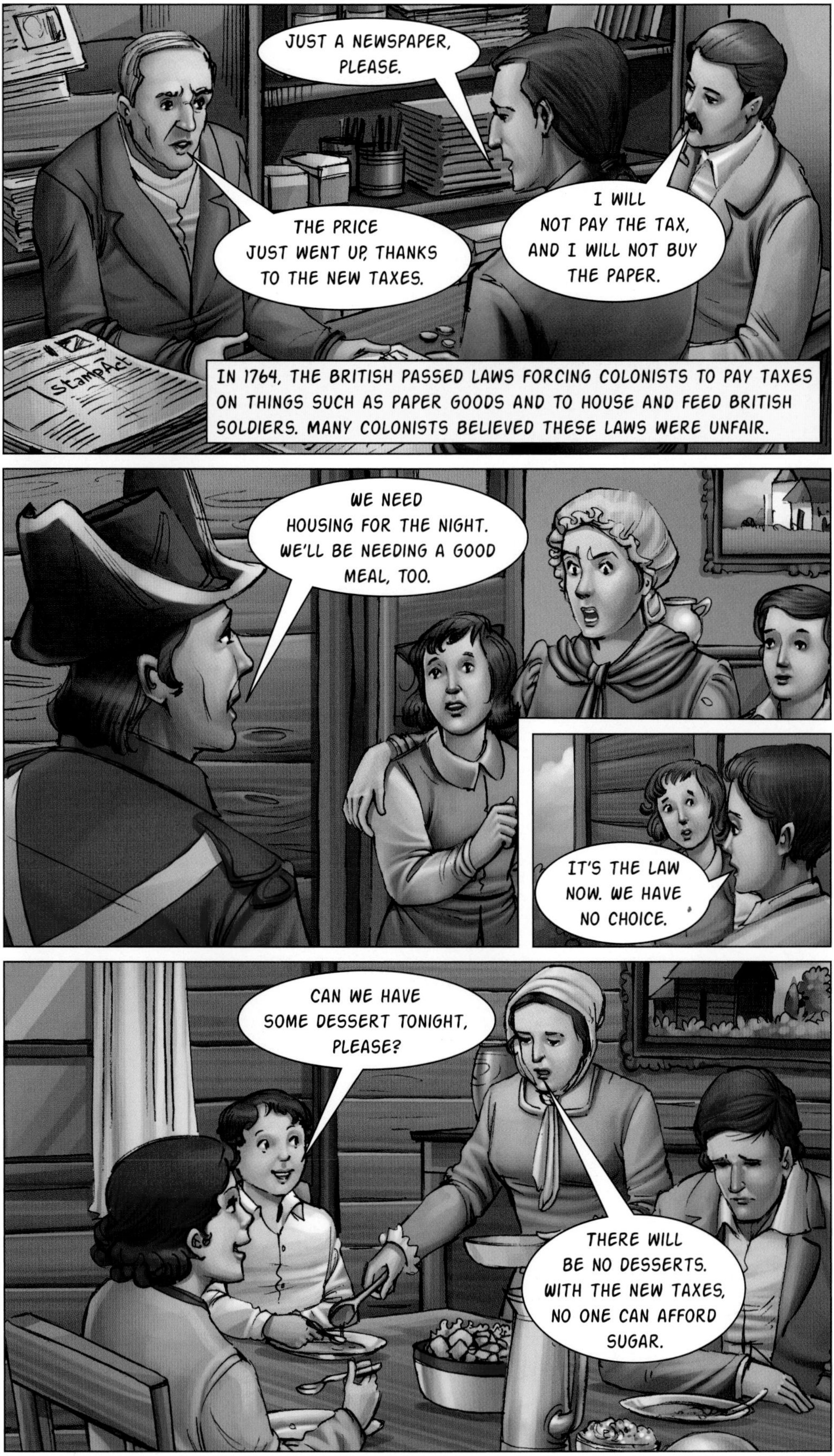
JUST A NEWSPAPER, PLEASE.
THE PRICE JUST WENT UP, THANKS TO THE NEW TAXES.
I WILL NOT PAY THE TAX, AND I WILL NOT BUY THE PAPER.
StampAct
IN 1764, THE BRITISH PASSED LAWS FORCING COLONISTS TO PAY TAXES ON THINGS SUCH AS PAPER GOODS AND TO HOUSE AND FEED BRITISH SOLDIERS. MANY COLONISTS BELIEVED THESE LAWS WERE UNFAIR.
WE NEED HOUSING FOR THE NIGHT. WE'LL BE NEEDING A GOOD MEAL, TOO.
IT'S THE LAW NOW. WE HAVE NO CHOICE.
CAN WE HAVE SOME DESSERT TONIGHT, PLEASE?
THERE WILL BE NO DESSERTS. WITH THE NEW TAXES, NO ONE CAN AFFORD SUGAR.

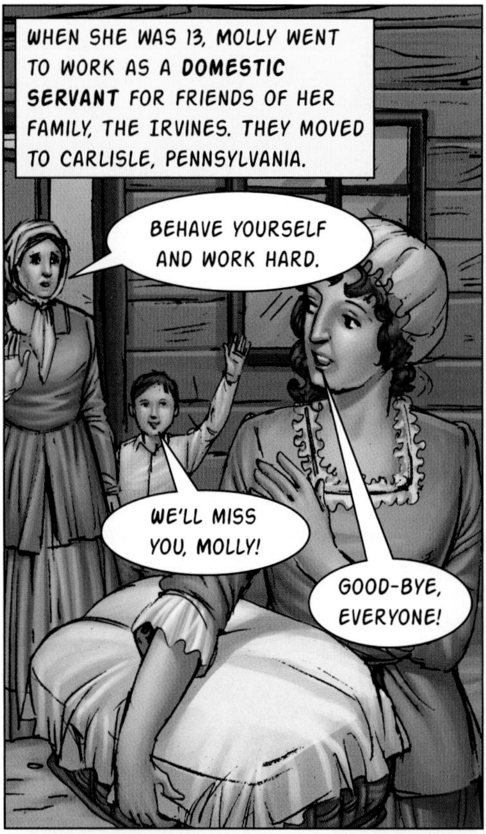
WHEN SHE WAS 13, MOLLY WENT TO WORK AS A **DOMESTIC SERVANT** FOR FRIENDS OF HER FAMILY, THE IRVINES. THEY MOVED TO CARLISLE, PENNSYLVANIA.
BEHAVE YOURSELF AND WORK HARD.
WE'LL MISS YOU, MOLLY!
GOOD-BYE, EVERYONE!

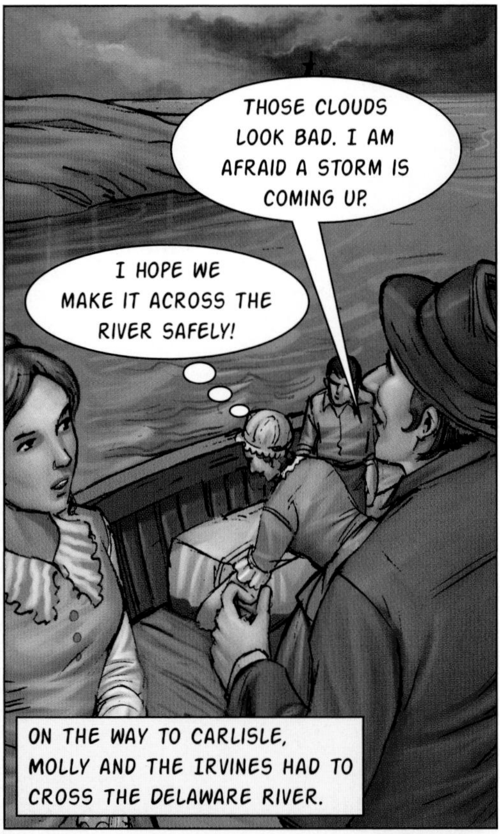
ON THE WAY TO CARLISLE, MOLLY AND THE IRVINES HAD TO CROSS THE DELAWARE RIVER.
THOSE CLOUDS LOOK BAD. I AM AFRAID A STORM IS COMING UP.
I HOPE WE MAKE IT ACROSS THE RIVER SAFELY!

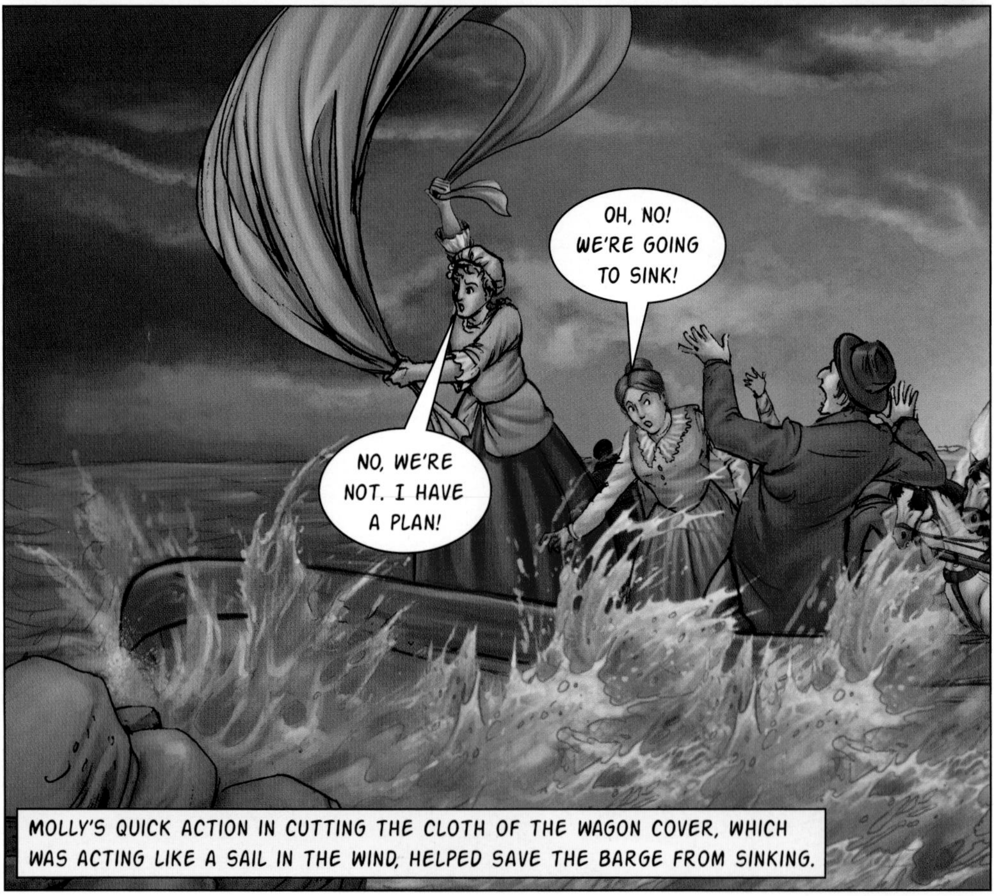
OH, NO! WE'RE GOING TO SINK!
NO, WE'RE NOT. I HAVE A PLAN!
MOLLY'S QUICK ACTION IN CUTTING THE CLOTH OF THE WAGON COVER, WHICH WAS ACTING LIKE A SAIL IN THE WIND, HELPED SAVE THE BARGE FROM SINKING.

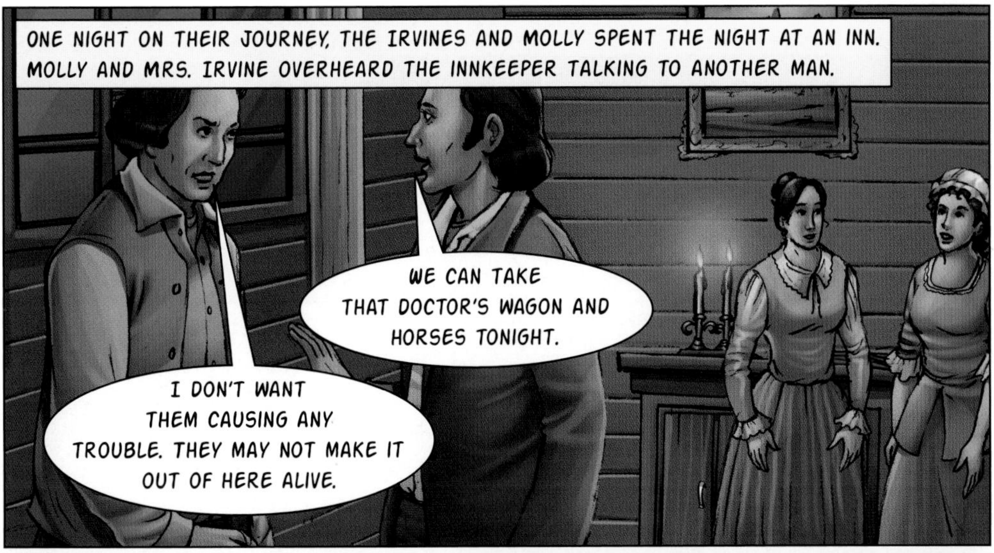
ONE NIGHT ON THEIR JOURNEY, THE IRVINES AND MOLLY SPENT THE NIGHT AT AN INN. MOLLY AND MRS. IRVINE OVERHEARD THE INNKEEPER TALKING TO ANOTHER MAN.
WE CAN TAKE THAT DOCTOR'S WAGON AND HORSES TONIGHT.
I DON'T WANT THEM CAUSING ANY TROUBLE. THEY MAY NOT MAKE IT OUT OF HERE ALIVE.

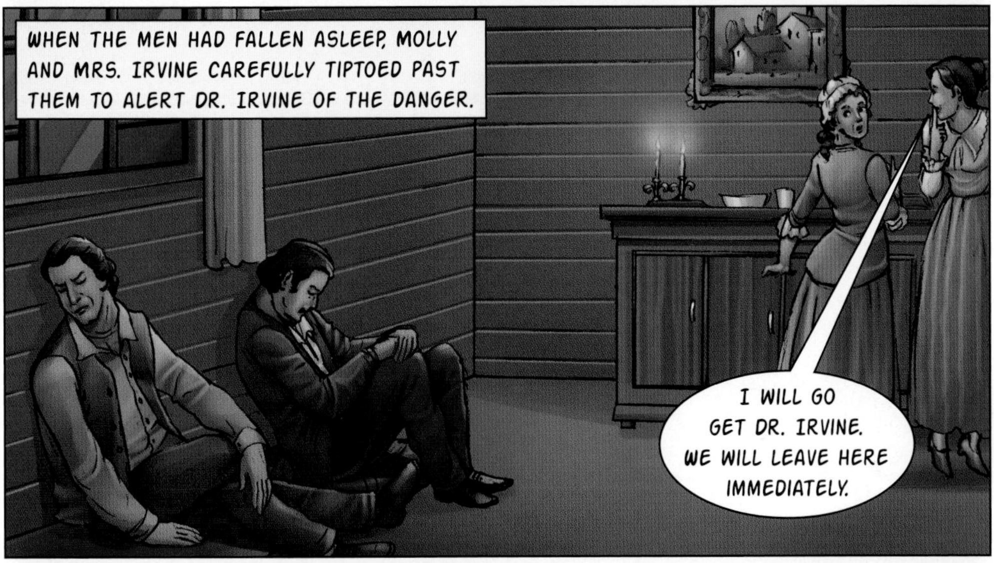
WHEN THE MEN HAD FALLEN ASLEEP, MOLLY AND MRS. IRVINE CAREFULLY TIPTOED PAST THEM TO ALERT DR. IRVINE OF THE DANGER.
I WILL GO GET DR. IRVINE. WE WILL LEAVE HERE IMMEDIATELY.

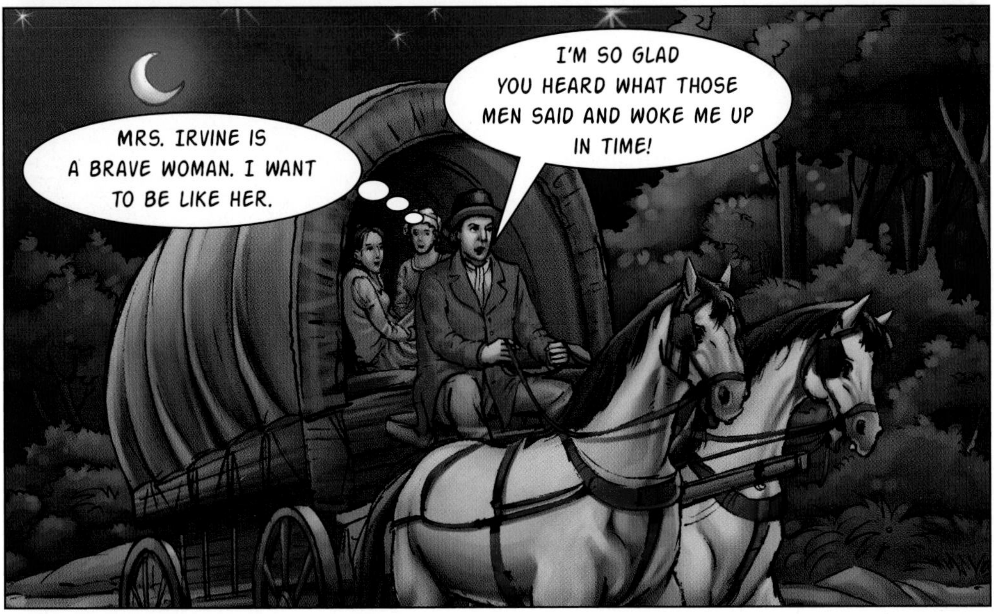
MRS. IRVINE IS A BRAVE WOMAN. I WANT TO BE LIKE HER.
I'M SO GLAD YOU HEARD WHAT THOSE MEN SAID AND WOKE ME UP IN TIME!

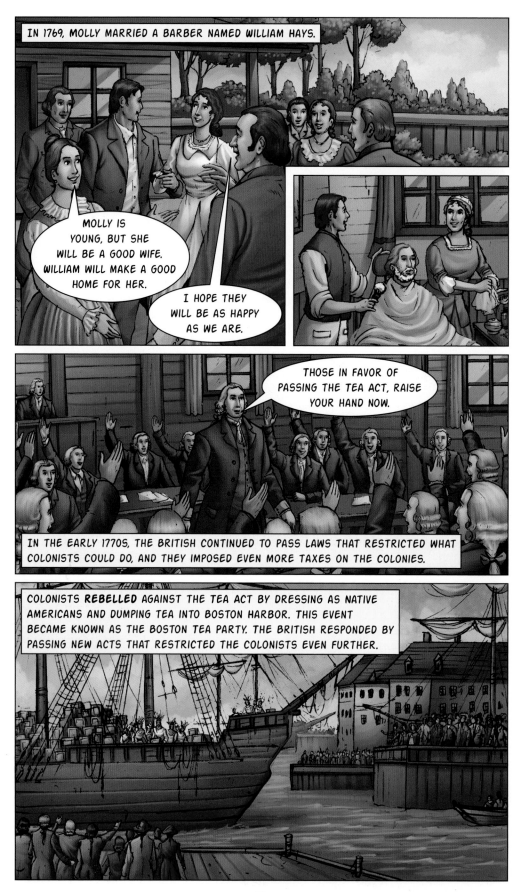

IN 1769, MOLLY MARRIED A BARBER NAMED WILLIAM HAYS.

MOLLY IS YOUNG, BUT SHE WILL BE A GOOD WIFE. WILLIAM WILL MAKE A GOOD HOME FOR HER.

I HOPE THEY WILL BE AS HAPPY AS WE ARE.

THOSE IN FAVOR OF PASSING THE TEA ACT, RAISE YOUR HAND NOW.

IN THE EARLY 1770S, THE BRITISH CONTINUED TO PASS LAWS THAT RESTRICTED WHAT COLONISTS COULD DO, AND THEY IMPOSED EVEN MORE TAXES ON THE COLONIES.

COLONISTS **REBELLED** AGAINST THE TEA ACT BY DRESSING AS NATIVE AMERICANS AND DUMPING TEA INTO BOSTON HARBOR. THIS EVENT BECAME KNOWN AS THE BOSTON TEA PARTY. THE BRITISH RESPONDED BY PASSING NEW ACTS THAT RESTRICTED THE COLONISTS EVEN FURTHER.

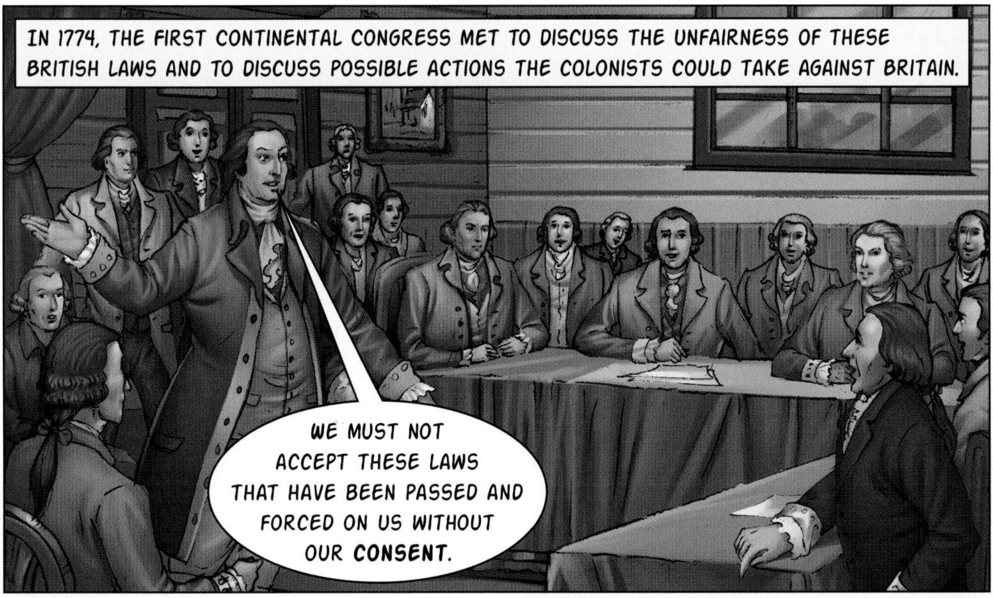
IN 1774, THE FIRST CONTINENTAL CONGRESS MET TO DISCUSS THE UNFAIRNESS OF THESE BRITISH LAWS AND TO DISCUSS POSSIBLE ACTIONS THE COLONISTS COULD TAKE AGAINST BRITAIN.
WE MUST NOT ACCEPT THESE LAWS THAT HAVE BEEN PASSED AND FORCED ON US WITHOUT OUR **CONSENT**.

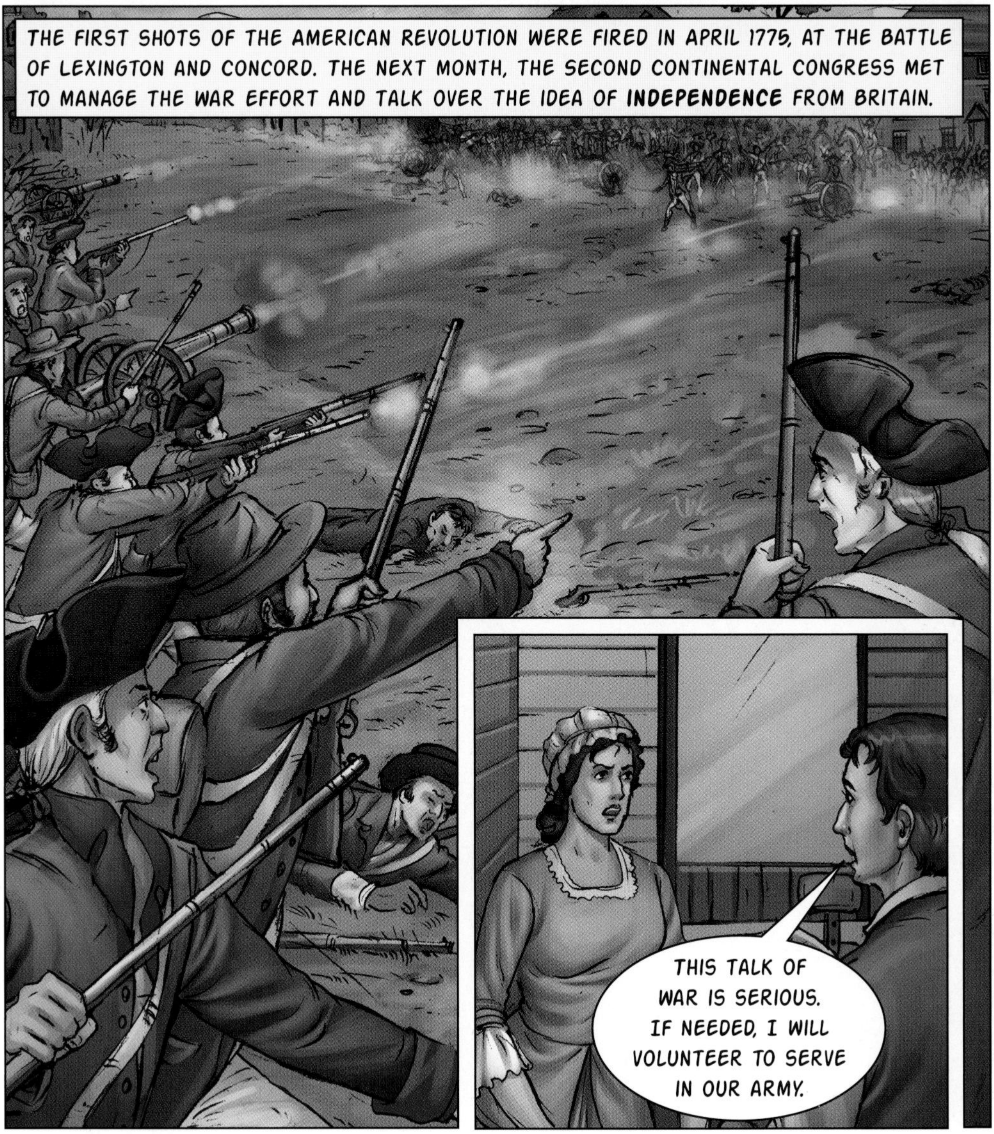
THE FIRST SHOTS OF THE AMERICAN REVOLUTION WERE FIRED IN APRIL 1775, AT THE BATTLE OF LEXINGTON AND CONCORD. THE NEXT MONTH, THE SECOND CONTINENTAL CONGRESS MET TO MANAGE THE WAR EFFORT AND TALK OVER THE IDEA OF **INDEPENDENCE** FROM BRITAIN.
THIS TALK OF WAR IS SERIOUS. IF NEEDED, I WILL VOLUNTEER TO SERVE IN OUR ARMY.

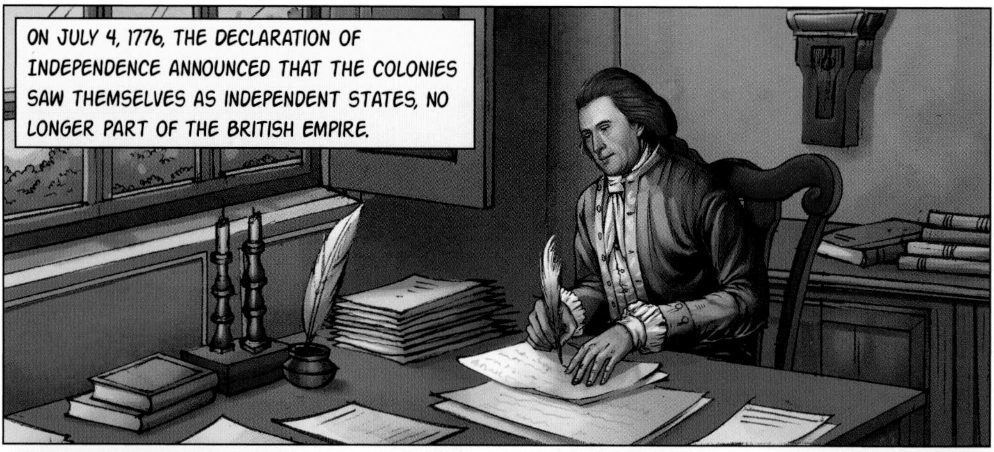
ON JULY 4, 1776, THE DECLARATION OF INDEPENDENCE ANNOUNCED THAT THE COLONIES SAW THEMSELVES AS INDEPENDENT STATES, NO LONGER PART OF THE BRITISH EMPIRE.

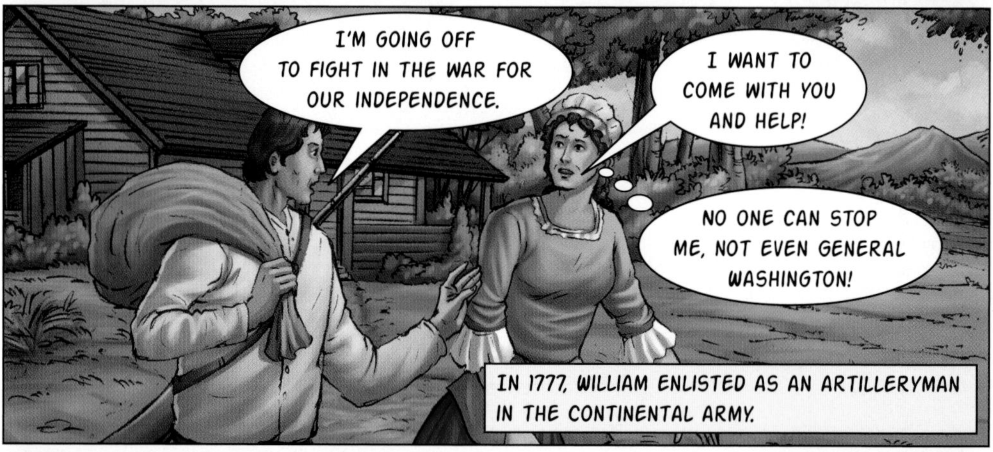
I'M GOING OFF TO FIGHT IN THE WAR FOR OUR INDEPENDENCE.
I WANT TO COME WITH YOU AND HELP!
NO ONE CAN STOP ME, NOT EVEN GENERAL WASHINGTON!
IN 1777, WILLIAM ENLISTED AS AN ARTILLERYMAN IN THE CONTINENTAL ARMY.

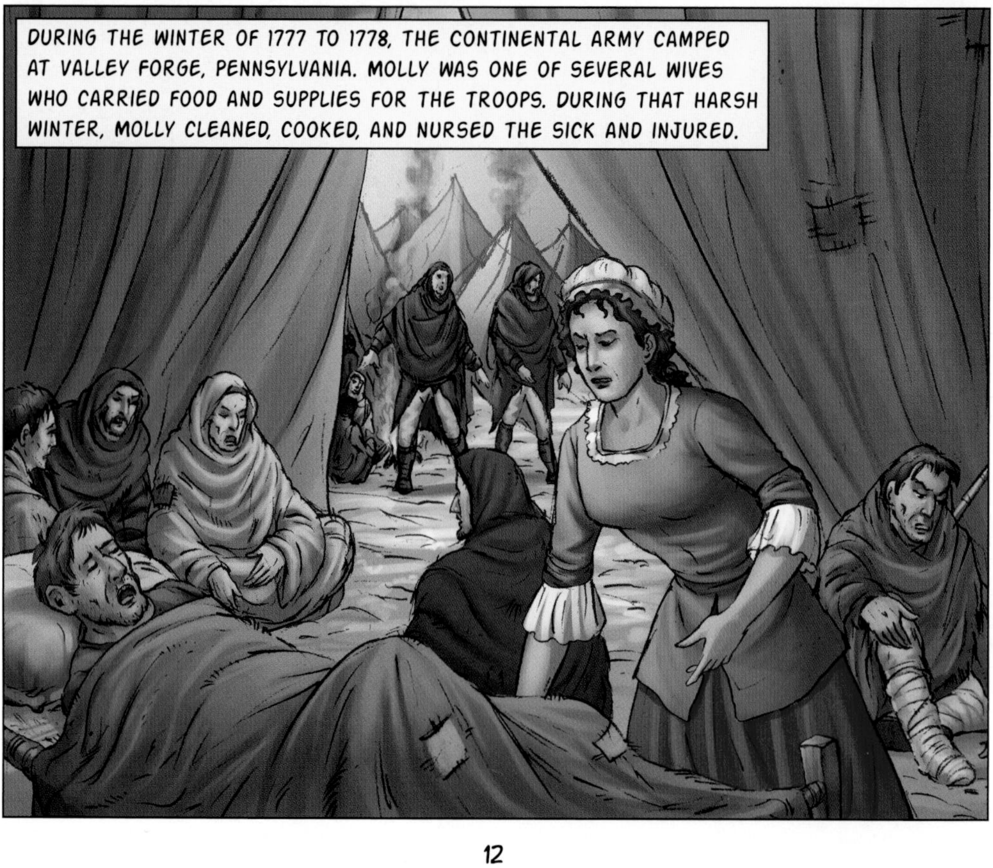
DURING THE WINTER OF 1777 TO 1778, THE CONTINENTAL ARMY CAMPED AT VALLEY FORGE, PENNSYLVANIA. MOLLY WAS ONE OF SEVERAL WIVES WHO CARRIED FOOD AND SUPPLIES FOR THE TROOPS. DURING THAT HARSH WINTER, MOLLY CLEANED, COOKED, AND NURSED THE SICK AND INJURED.

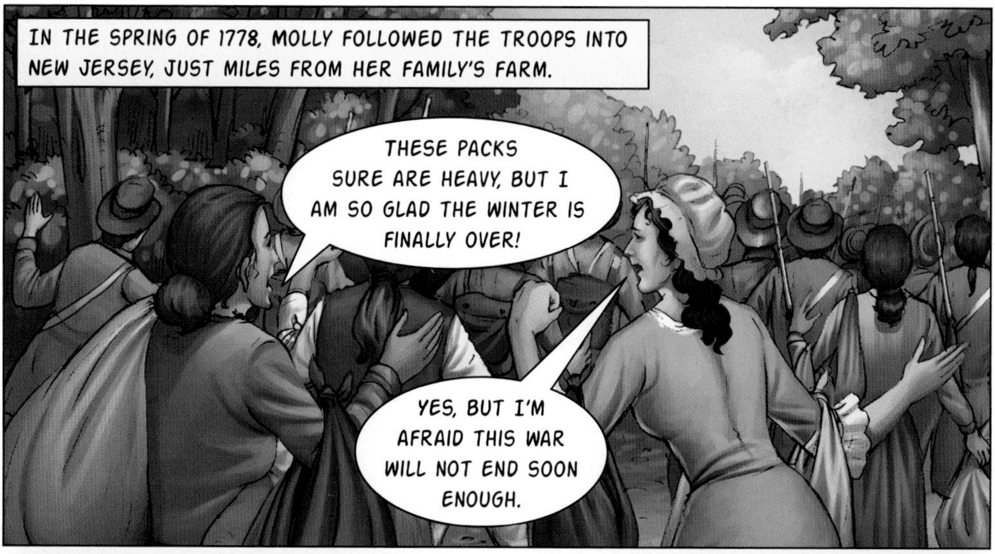
IN THE SPRING OF 1778, MOLLY FOLLOWED THE TROOPS INTO NEW JERSEY, JUST MILES FROM HER FAMILY'S FARM.
THESE PACKS SURE ARE HEAVY, BUT I AM SO GLAD THE WINTER IS FINALLY OVER!
YES, BUT I'M AFRAID THIS WAR WILL NOT END SOON ENOUGH.

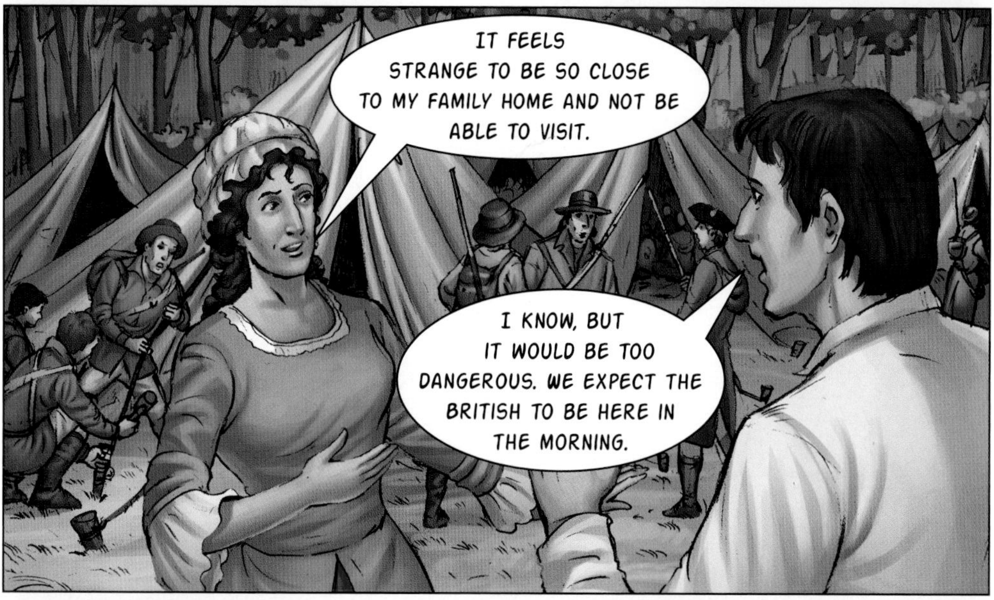
IT FEELS STRANGE TO BE SO CLOSE TO MY FAMILY HOME AND NOT BE ABLE TO VISIT.
I KNOW, BUT IT WOULD BE TOO DANGEROUS. WE EXPECT THE BRITISH TO BE HERE IN THE MORNING.

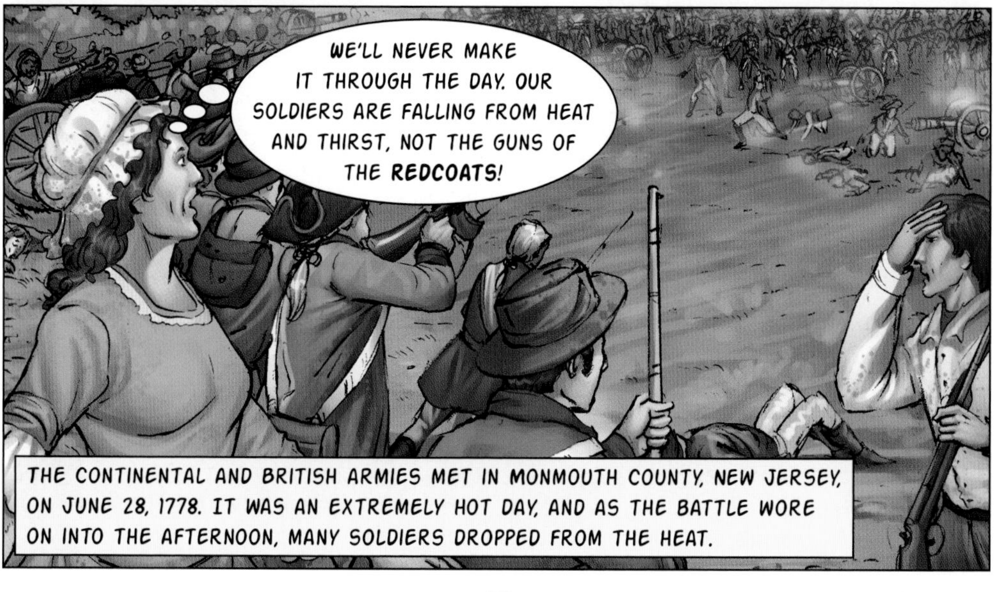
WE'LL NEVER MAKE IT THROUGH THE DAY. OUR SOLDIERS ARE FALLING FROM HEAT AND THIRST, NOT THE GUNS OF THE **REDCOATS**!
THE CONTINENTAL AND BRITISH ARMIES MET IN MONMOUTH COUNTY, NEW JERSEY, ON JUNE 28, 1778. IT WAS AN EXTREMELY HOT DAY, AND AS THE BATTLE WORE ON INTO THE AFTERNOON, MANY SOLDIERS DROPPED FROM THE HEAT.

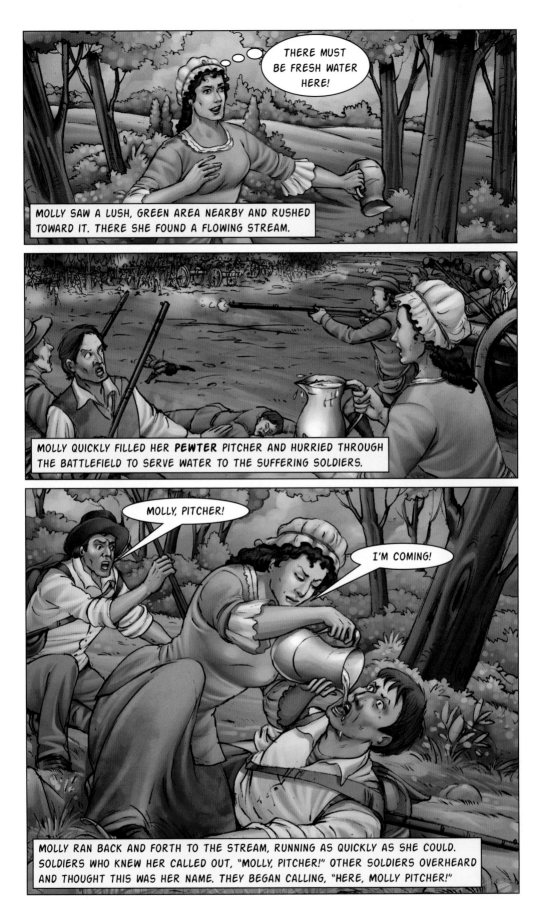

THERE MUST BE FRESH WATER HERE!

MOLLY SAW A LUSH, GREEN AREA NEARBY AND RUSHED TOWARD IT. THERE SHE FOUND A FLOWING STREAM.

MOLLY QUICKLY FILLED HER **PEWTER** PITCHER AND HURRIED THROUGH THE BATTLEFIELD TO SERVE WATER TO THE SUFFERING SOLDIERS.

MOLLY, PITCHER!

I'M COMING!

MOLLY RAN BACK AND FORTH TO THE STREAM, RUNNING AS QUICKLY AS SHE COULD. SOLDIERS WHO KNEW HER CALLED OUT, "MOLLY, PITCHER!" OTHER SOLDIERS OVERHEARD AND THOUGHT THIS WAS HER NAME. THEY BEGAN CALLING, "HERE, MOLLY PITCHER!"

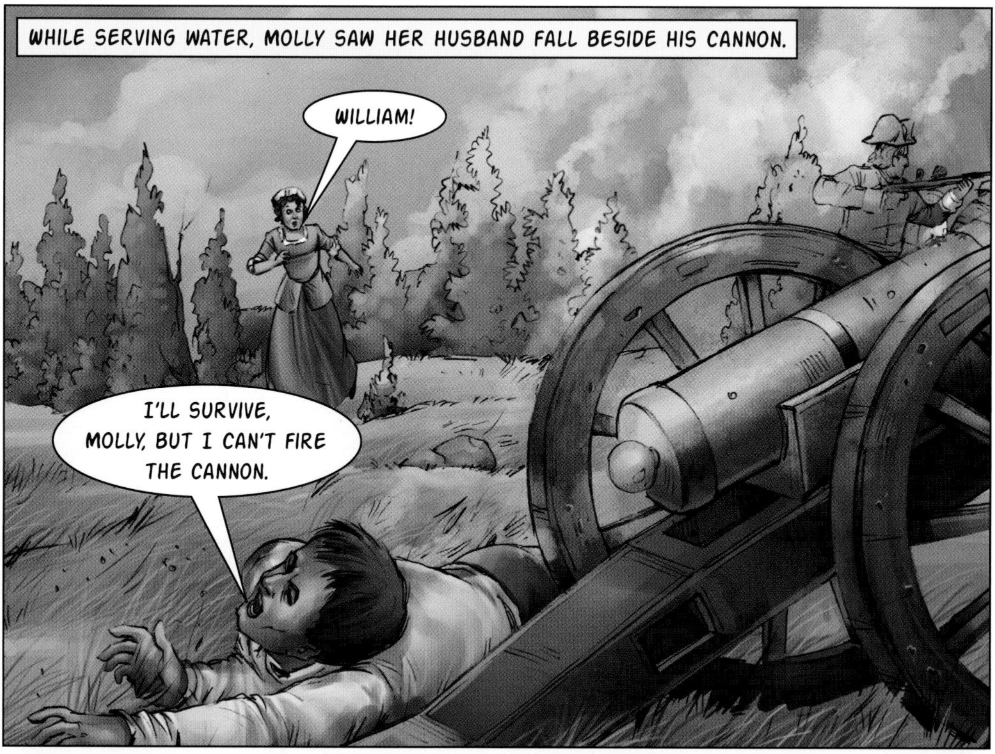
WHILE SERVING WATER, MOLLY SAW HER HUSBAND FALL BESIDE HIS CANNON.
WILLIAM!
I'LL SURVIVE, MOLLY, BUT I CAN'T FIRE THE CANNON.

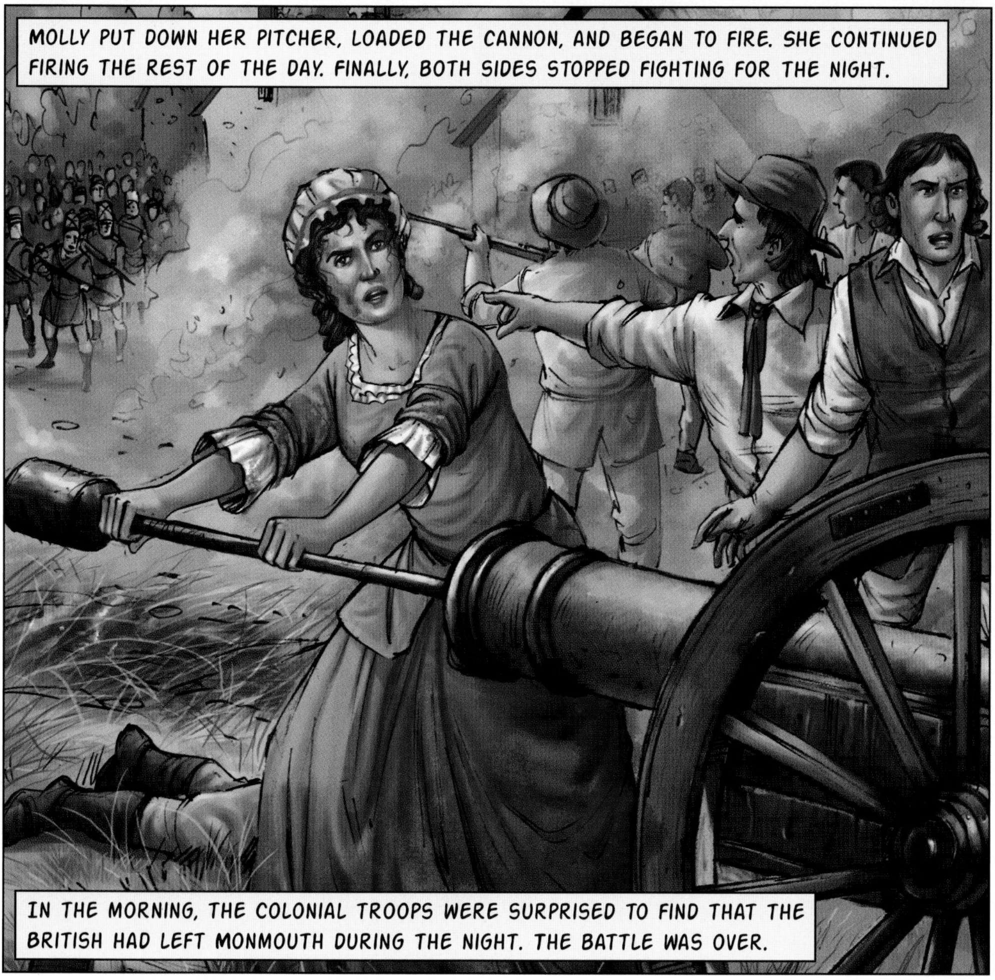
MOLLY PUT DOWN HER PITCHER, LOADED THE CANNON, AND BEGAN TO FIRE. SHE CONTINUED FIRING THE REST OF THE DAY. FINALLY, BOTH SIDES STOPPED FIGHTING FOR THE NIGHT.
IN THE MORNING, THE COLONIAL TROOPS WERE SURPRISED TO FIND THAT THE BRITISH HAD LEFT MONMOUTH DURING THE NIGHT. THE BATTLE WAS OVER.

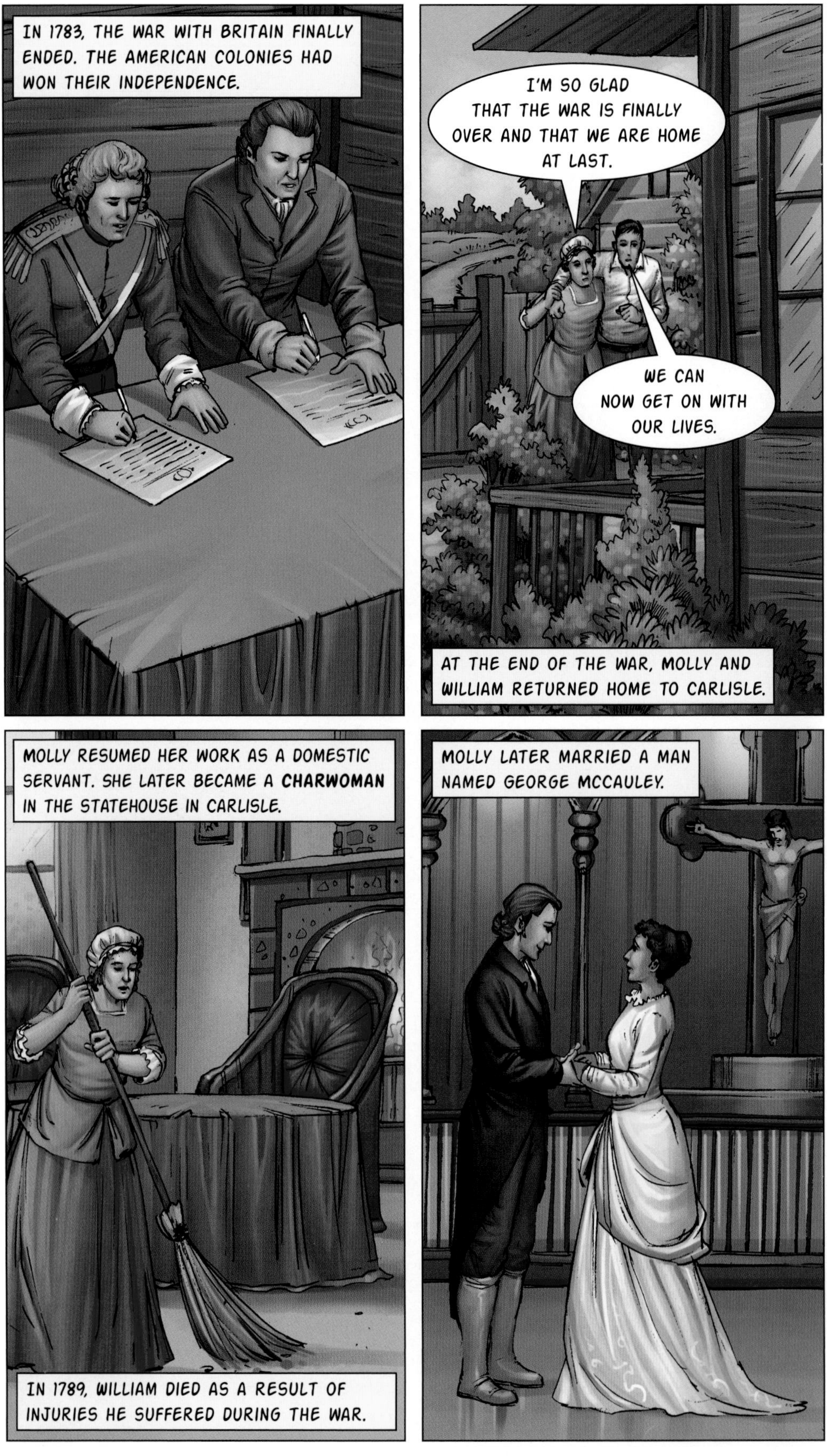
IN 1783, THE WAR WITH BRITAIN FINALLY ENDED. THE AMERICAN COLONIES HAD WON THEIR INDEPENDENCE.
I'M SO GLAD THAT THE WAR IS FINALLY OVER AND THAT WE ARE HOME AT LAST.
WE CAN NOW GET ON WITH OUR LIVES.
AT THE END OF THE WAR, MOLLY AND WILLIAM RETURNED HOME TO CARLISLE.
MOLLY RESUMED HER WORK AS A DOMESTIC SERVANT. SHE LATER BECAME A **CHARWOMAN** IN THE STATEHOUSE IN CARLISLE.
IN 1789, WILLIAM DIED AS A RESULT OF INJURIES HE SUFFERED DURING THE WAR.
MOLLY LATER MARRIED A MAN NAMED GEORGE MCCAULEY.

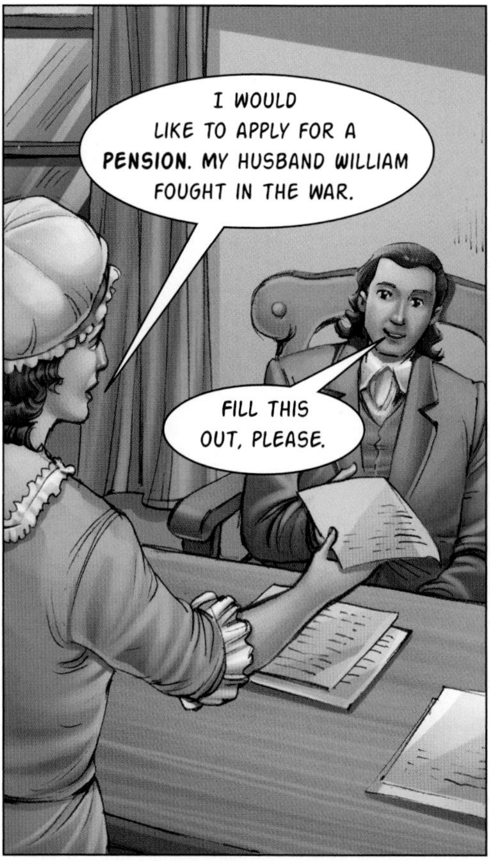
I WOULD LIKE TO APPLY FOR A **PENSION**. MY HUSBAND WILLIAM FOUGHT IN THE WAR.
FILL THIS OUT, PLEASE.

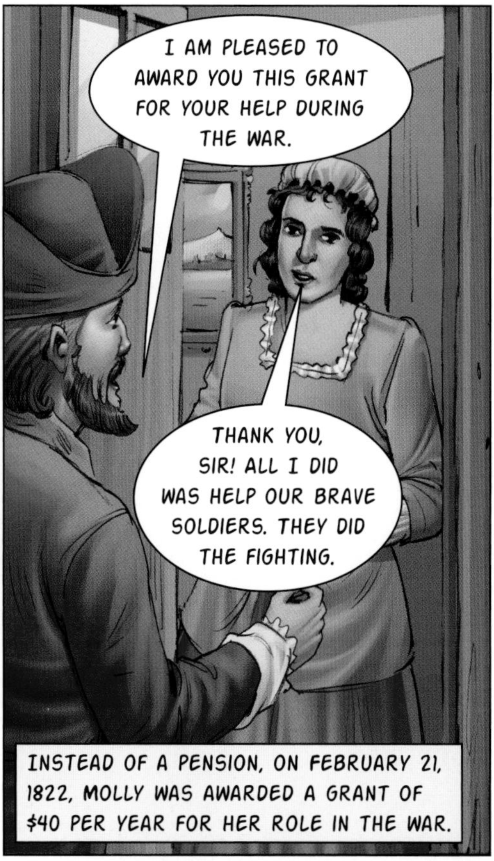
I AM PLEASED TO AWARD YOU THIS GRANT FOR YOUR HELP DURING THE WAR.
THANK YOU, SIR! ALL I DID WAS HELP OUR BRAVE SOLDIERS. THEY DID THE FIGHTING.
INSTEAD OF A PENSION, ON FEBRUARY 21, 1822, MOLLY WAS AWARDED A GRANT OF $40 PER YEAR FOR HER ROLE IN THE WAR.

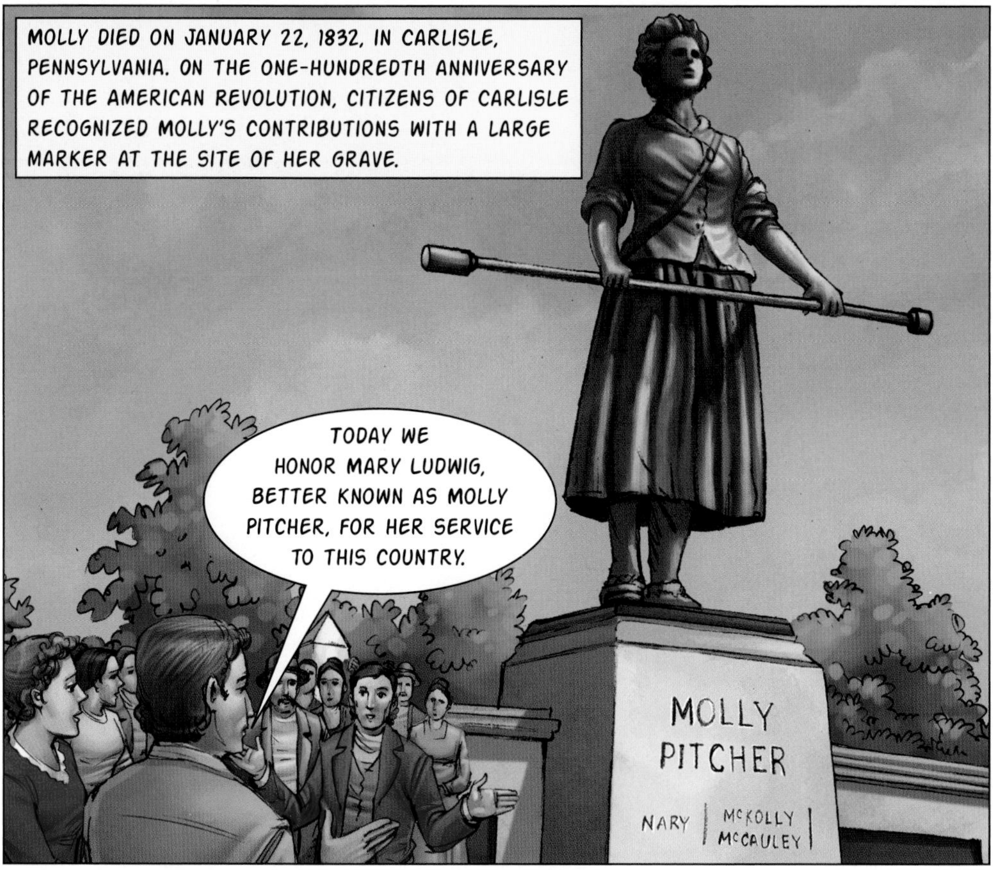
MOLLY DIED ON JANUARY 22, 1832, IN CARLISLE, PENNSYLVANIA. ON THE ONE-HUNDREDTH ANNIVERSARY OF THE AMERICAN REVOLUTION, CITIZENS OF CARLISLE RECOGNIZED MOLLY'S CONTRIBUTIONS WITH A LARGE MARKER AT THE SITE OF HER GRAVE.
TODAY WE HONOR MARY LUDWIG, BETTER KNOWN AS MOLLY PITCHER, FOR HER SERVICE TO THIS COUNTRY.
MOLLY PITCHER
NARY | McKOLLY McCAULEY |

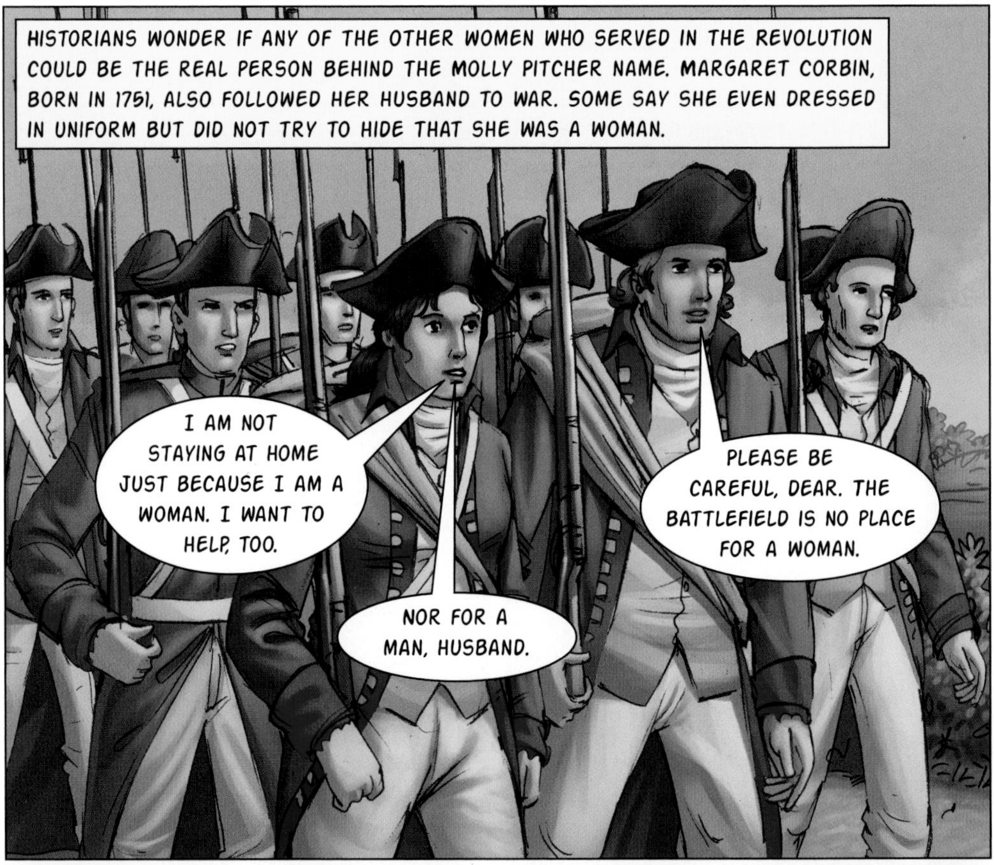
HISTORIANS WONDER IF ANY OF THE OTHER WOMEN WHO SERVED IN THE REVOLUTION COULD BE THE REAL PERSON BEHIND THE MOLLY PITCHER NAME. MARGARET CORBIN, BORN IN 1751, ALSO FOLLOWED HER HUSBAND TO WAR. SOME SAY SHE EVEN DRESSED IN UNIFORM BUT DID NOT TRY TO HIDE THAT SHE WAS A WOMAN.
I AM NOT STAYING AT HOME JUST BECAUSE I AM A WOMAN. I WANT TO HELP, TOO.
PLEASE BE CAREFUL, DEAR. THE BATTLEFIELD IS NO PLACE FOR A WOMAN.
NOR FOR A MAN, HUSBAND.

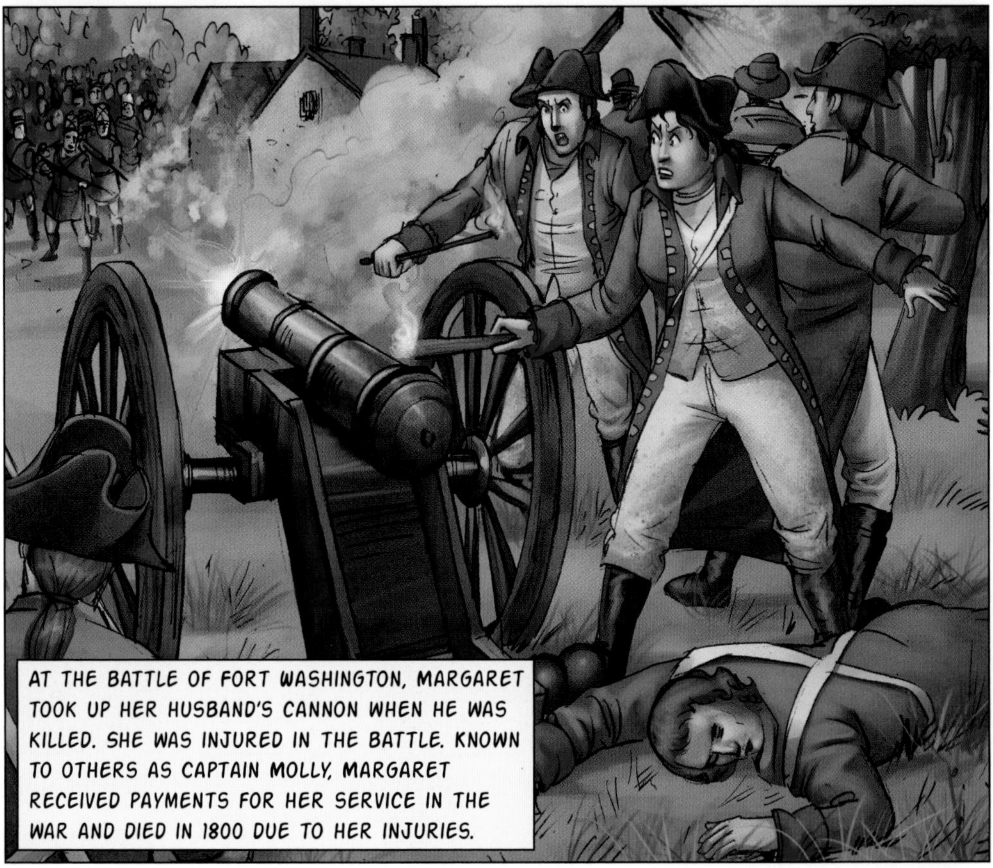
AT THE BATTLE OF FORT WASHINGTON, MARGARET TOOK UP HER HUSBAND'S CANNON WHEN HE WAS KILLED. SHE WAS INJURED IN THE BATTLE. KNOWN TO OTHERS AS CAPTAIN MOLLY, MARGARET RECEIVED PAYMENTS FOR HER SERVICE IN THE WAR AND DIED IN 1800 DUE TO HER INJURIES.

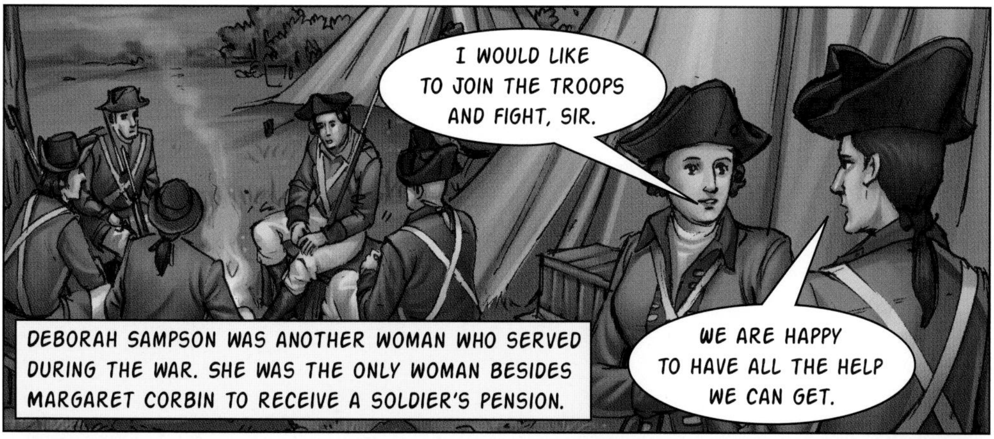
I WOULD LIKE TO JOIN THE TROOPS AND FIGHT, SIR.
DEBORAH SAMPSON WAS ANOTHER WOMAN WHO SERVED DURING THE WAR. SHE WAS THE ONLY WOMAN BESIDES MARGARET CORBIN TO RECEIVE A SOLDIER'S PENSION.
WE ARE HAPPY TO HAVE ALL THE HELP WE CAN GET.

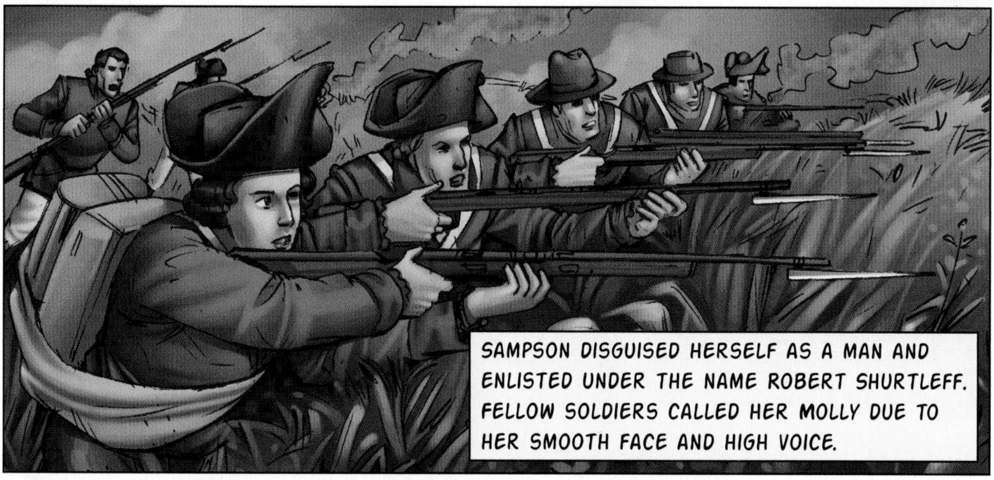
SAMPSON DISGUISED HERSELF AS A MAN AND ENLISTED UNDER THE NAME ROBERT SHURTLEFF. FELLOW SOLDIERS CALLED HER MOLLY DUE TO HER SMOOTH FACE AND HIGH VOICE.

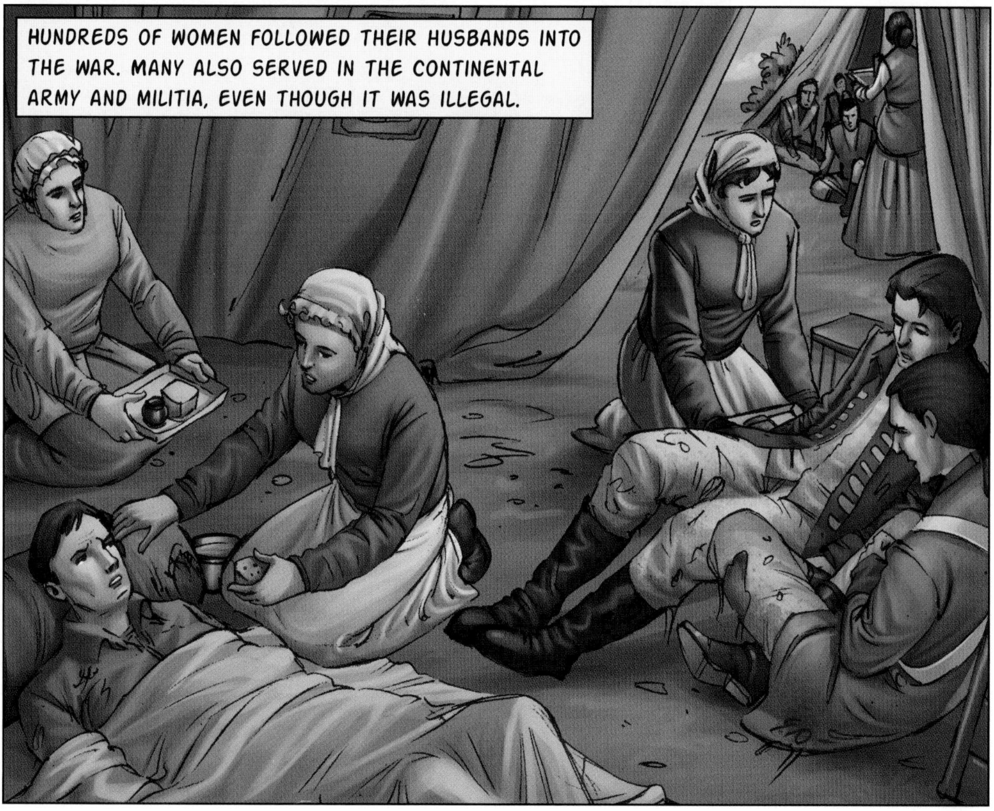
HUNDREDS OF WOMEN FOLLOWED THEIR HUSBANDS INTO THE WAR. MANY ALSO SERVED IN THE CONTINENTAL ARMY AND MILITIA, EVEN THOUGH IT WAS ILLEGAL.

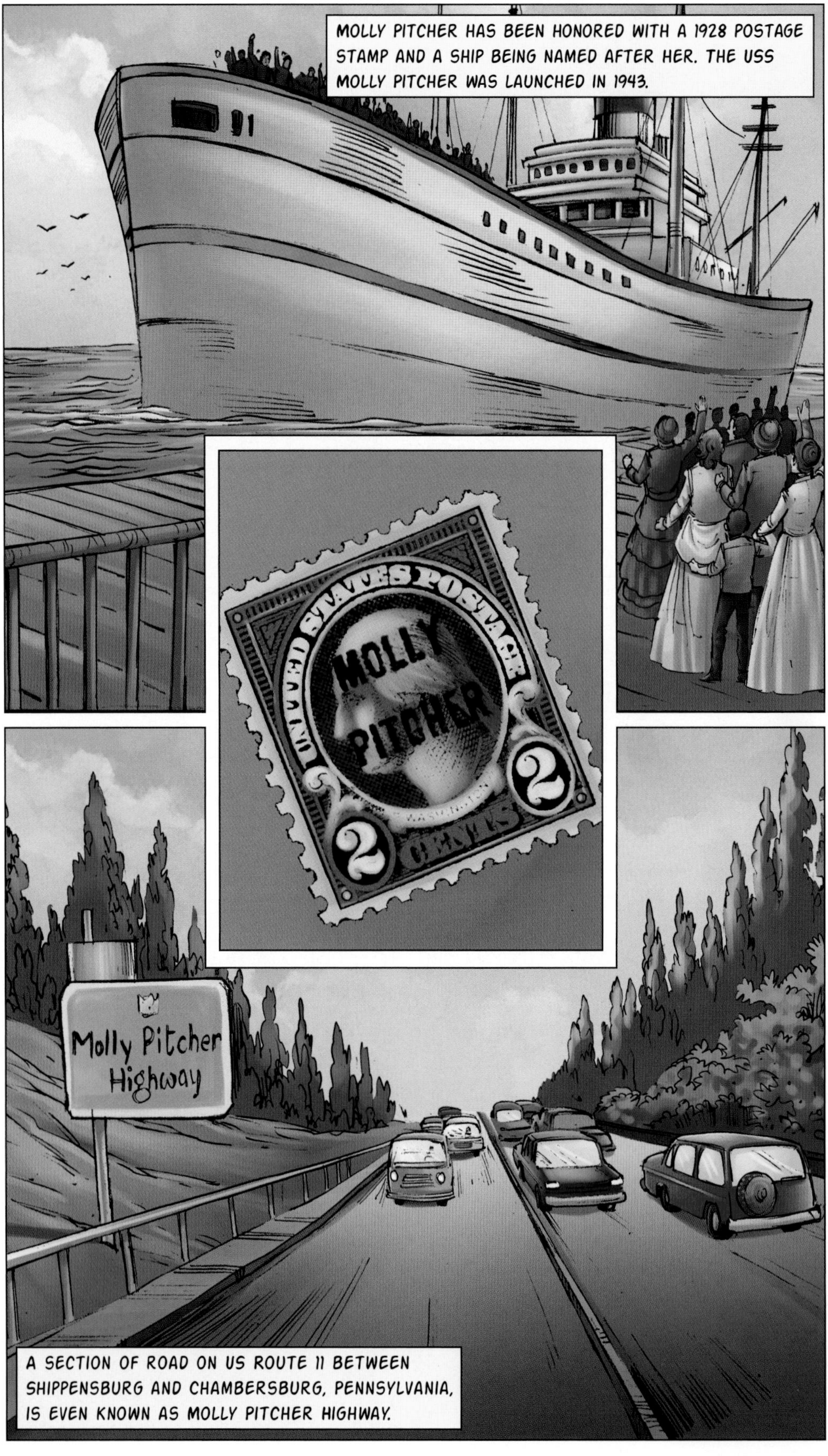
MOLLY PITCHER HAS BEEN HONORED WITH A 1928 POSTAGE STAMP AND A SHIP BEING NAMED AFTER HER. THE USS MOLLY PITCHER WAS LAUNCHED IN 1943.
UNITED STATES POSTAGE
MOLLY PITCHER
2 CENTS
Molly Pitcher Highway
A SECTION OF ROAD ON US ROUTE 11 BETWEEN SHIPPENSBURG AND CHAMBERSBURG, PENNSYLVANIA, IS EVEN KNOWN AS MOLLY PITCHER HIGHWAY.

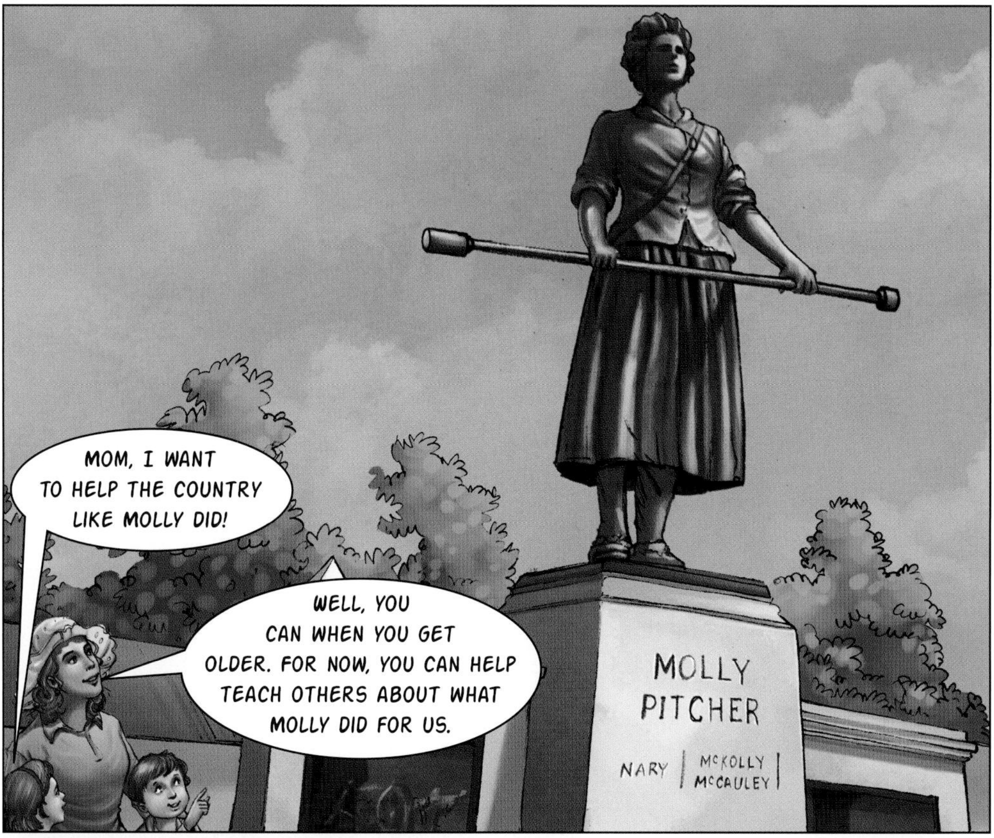
MOM, I WANT TO HELP THE COUNTRY LIKE MOLLY DID!
WELL, YOU CAN WHEN YOU GET OLDER. FOR NOW, YOU CAN HELP TEACH OTHERS ABOUT WHAT MOLLY DID FOR US.
MOLLY PITCHER
NARY
McKOLLY McCAULEY

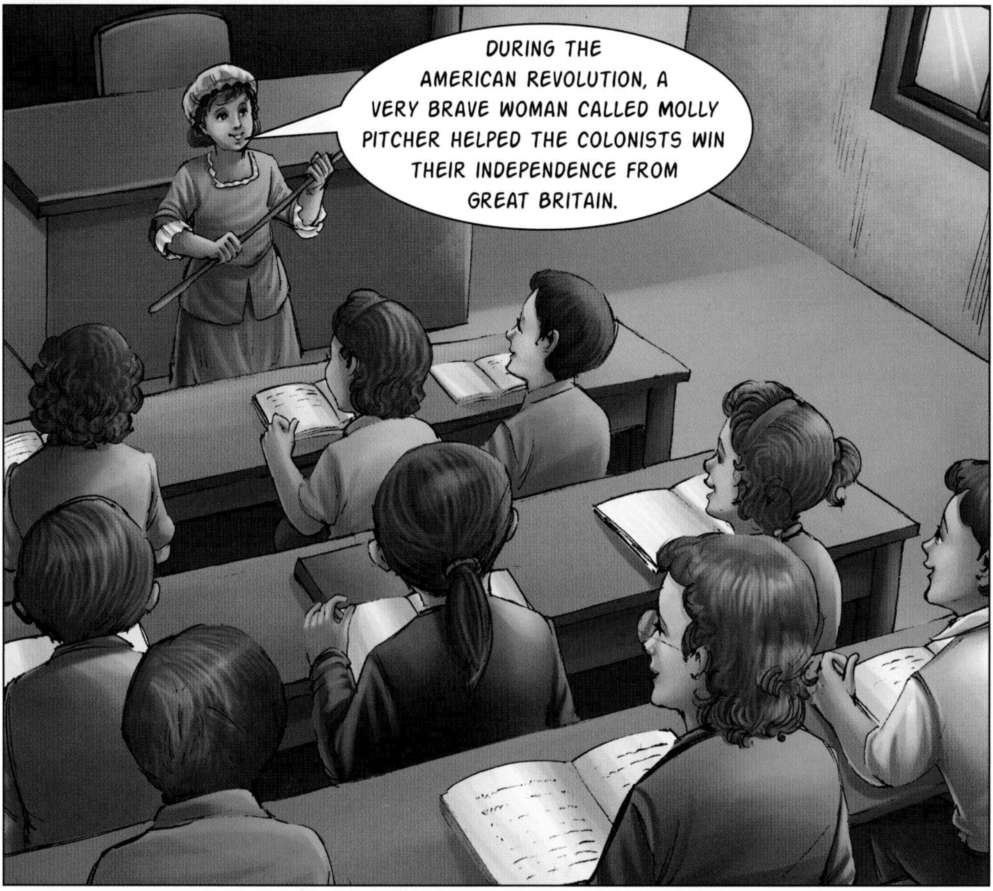
DURING THE AMERICAN REVOLUTION, A VERY BRAVE WOMAN CALLED MOLLY PITCHER HELPED THE COLONISTS WIN THEIR INDEPENDENCE FROM GREAT BRITAIN.

Timeline

October 1754   Mary Ludwig is born near Trenton, New Jersey.

1764   The Sugar Act and Currency Act are passed in Britain, beginning Colonial opposition.

1765   The Quartering Act and Stamp Act are passed, and colonists begin organized protests.

c. 1767   Molly leaves home to work as a domestic servant for Dr. and Mrs. Irvine.

1768   British troops arrive in Boston.

1769   Molly marries William Hays.

1773   After the Tea Act passes, colonists carry out the Boston Tea Party.

1774   The First Continental Congress meets.

April 1775   The American Revolution begins with the Battle of Lexington and Concord.

May 1775   The Second Continental Congress meets.

July 1776   The Declaration of Independence announces the colonists' plan to separate from Great Britain.

1777   William Hays enlists in the Continental army.

December 1777   Colonial troops camp at Valley Forge, Pennsylvania. Molly comes along with William to help.

June 1778   The colonists win the Battle of Monmouth, in New Jersey, thanks to Molly's help serving water to soldiers and taking over her husband's cannon when he is injured.

September 1783   The American Revolution ends with the signing of the Treaty of Paris.

1789   William Hays dies due to injuries suffered during the war.

February 1822   Molly is awarded a yearly grant for her services in the American Revolution.

January 1832   Molly dies in Carlisle, Pennsylvania.

1876   Citizens of Carlisle honor Molly Pitcher with a grave marker at the one-hundredth anniversary of the American Revolution.

Glossary

American Revolution (uh-MER-uh-ken reh-vuh-LOO-shun)
Battles that soldiers from the colonies fought against
Britain for freedom, from 1775 to 1783.

battlefield (BA-tel-feeld) A place where a battle is fought.

charwoman (CHAHR-wu-men) A cleaning woman in a
large building.

consent (kun-SENT) Approval or permission.

disguised (dis-GYZD) Wore a costume or outfit to hide
one's identity.

domestic servant (duh-MES-tik SER-vint) A person who is
employed to work in a household.

feminine (FEH-muh-nun) Like a woman.

independence (in-dih-PEN-dents) Freedom from the control
or support of other people.

injured (IN-jurd) Harmed or hurt.

military (MIH-luh-ter-ee) The part of the government, such as
the army or navy, that keeps its citizens safe.

pension (PEN-shun) Money paid when a person retires
from a job.

pewter (PYOO-tur) A dull, bluish-gray metal.

rebelled (rih-BELD) Disobeyed the people or country
in charge.

redcoats (RED-kohts) A slang term for British soldiers
because of these soldiers' bright red uniform coats.

Index

WebSites

Due to the changing nature of Internet links, PowerKids Press has developed an online list of websites related to the subject of this book. This site is updated regularly. Please use this link to access the list:

www.powerkidslinks.com/jgam/pitch/